AF147542

1 Match.

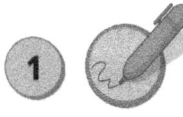

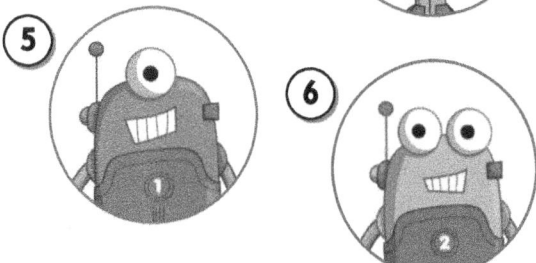

a My name's Katy.

b Hello. I'm Captain Conrad.

c I'm PROD 1.

d I'm President Pop. Welcome to Space Island.

e Hello, I'm PROD 2.

f I'm Kim.

2 Draw and write about yourself.

Hello.

My name's _____.

I'm (age) _____.

3 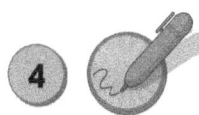 Listen, join the dots and write.

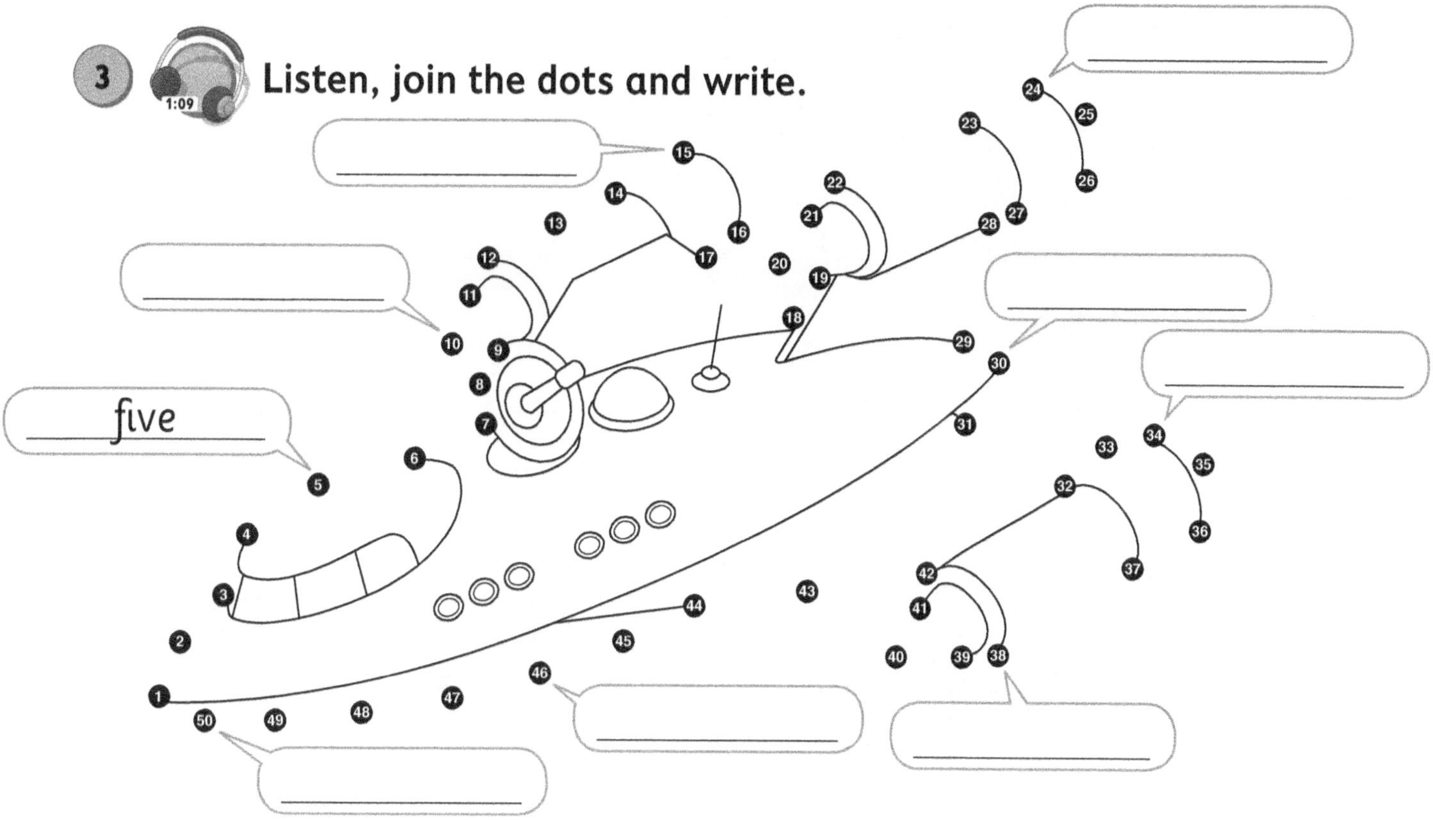

_____

_____

_____

_____

_____

_____five

_____

_____

4 Circle and write the days of the week.

w	s	t	j	o	a	w	t	m
m	o	n	d	a	y	e	h	k
s	f	t	o	a	b	d	u	l
x	w	y	q	o	i	n	r	e
s	u	n	d	a	y	e	s	o
a	d	f	c	n	m	s	d	y
e	b	z	f	r	i	d	a	y
s	a	t	u	r	d	a	y	w
t	u	e	s	d	a	y	t	v

_____Monday_____

_____

_____

_____

_____

_____

_____

Today is _____. My favourite day is _____.

1 Nature

1 Match.

flowers   insects   sun   birds

pond   rock   animal

2 Now colour.

3  **Listen, draw and colour.**

4 **Look and write.**

1 ___There's___ a blue pond. 2 _____ yellow flowers.

3 _____ a brown rock. 4 _____ a purple animal.

5 _____ pink insects. 6 _____ blue birds.

5 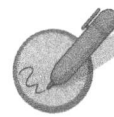 **Look and write.**

1 There ___are seven___ birds.   2 There _____ mushrooms.

3 There _____ rocks.   4 There _____ animals.

5 There _____ trees.   6 There _____ clouds.

7 There _____ pond.

6 **Tell the class.**

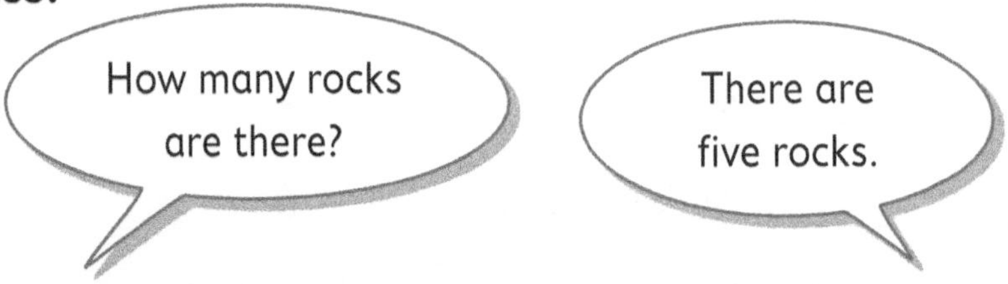

How many rocks
are there?

There are
five rocks.

7  **Look, match and write.**

1 The white horse

2 Two small birds

3 The flower and the mushroom

_____   _____

8  **Listen and tick (✓).**

  ✓

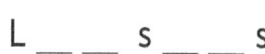

9  **Listen, write and say.**

Tr _e_ _e_ s, tr __ __ s, tr __ __ s.   L __ __ s __ __ s

Gr __ __ n, gr __ __ n, tr __ __ s.   Thr __ __ gr __ __ n tr __ __ s.

Thr __ __ gr __ __ n tr __ __ s.

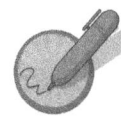 **Look and read. Then tick (✓) or cross (✗).**

1 There's a pond. ✓ **2** There's a sun. ☐

3 There are two birds. ☐ **4** There are six insects. ☐

5 There's a tifftiff plant. ☐

11 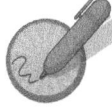 **Number the pictures.**

Is this a tifftiff?

a ☐

It's orange.

b 1

Look! It's a tifftiff plant!

c ☐

It isn't funny!

d ☐

It isn't a tifftiff!

e ☐

Help! I'm in the pond!

f ☐

(12)  **Draw and write.**

(1)  **+**  **= 6**

(2)  **–** **= 4**

(3)  **+** **= 7**

(4)  **–** **= 2**

1   Four insects plus _____two insects_____ equals six.

2   Seven mushrooms minus _____ equals four.

3   Four clouds plus _____ equals seven.

4   Six flowers minus _____ equals two.

(13)  **Solve the number puzzle.**

Five birds plus two cats.

How many legs? _____

(14)  **Complete the sums.**

a   11 + _2_ = 13

b   20 – ___ = 13

c   12 + ___ = 13

d   18 – ___ = 13

15 Complete the crossword.

1

2

```
      ¹t
       r
       e
       e
       s
```

²

³

3

4 **5**

8

6 **7**

4

5

6

7

8

16 Look and write.

1   There ___'s one___ tree.

2   There _____ rocks.

3   There _____ insects.

4   There _____ bird.

5   There _____ clouds.

6   There _____ mushrooms.

7   There _____ flowers.

17 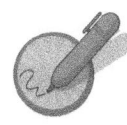 What's in your favourite park? Circle.

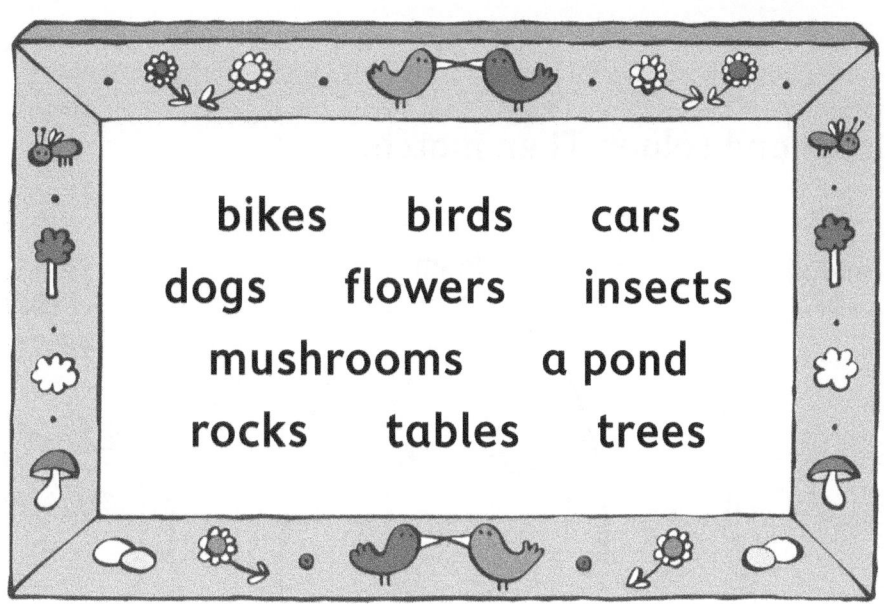

bikes   birds   cars

dogs   flowers   insects

mushrooms   a pond

rocks   tables   trees

18 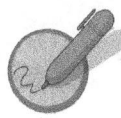 Look and write.

In my favourite park there's a 🏞️ ¹ _pond_

and there are 🪨 ² _____. There are

🌳 ³ _____ and 🐦 ⁴ _____.

There are a lot of 🌸 ⁵ _____. I love my park.

19 Write about your favourite park. Then tell the class.

In my favourite park, there's _____ and there are _____.

There are a lot of _____.

2 Me

1  **Listen and colour. Then match.**

Grandad   Mum   Peter

blonde hair
red hair
green eyes

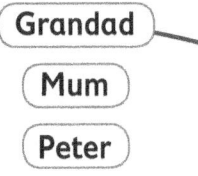
Grandad
Mum
Peter

blue eyes
white moustache
small glasses
short beard

2 **Write. Use the words in the box.**

| beard blonde eyes green hair moustache small |

1   Grandad has got a short ____beard____ and a white _____.

    He's got _____ eyes and _____ glasses.

2   Mum's got _____ hair.

3   Peter has got red _____.

4   Mum and Peter have got blue _____.

3  **Choose, draw and write.**

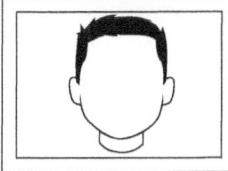

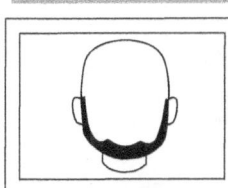

I've got _____.

_____

I haven't got _____.

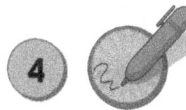 **4** **Look and write.**

He's got	She's got
He hasn't got	She hasn't got

1 _____He's got_____ long hair.

2 _____ a moustache.

3 _____ glasses.

4 _____ a beard.

5 _____She's got_____ long hair.

6 _____ glasses.

7 _____ a moustache.

8 _____ a beard.

5 **Listen and draw.**

Have you got big teeth?

Yes, I have.

Zig

Zog

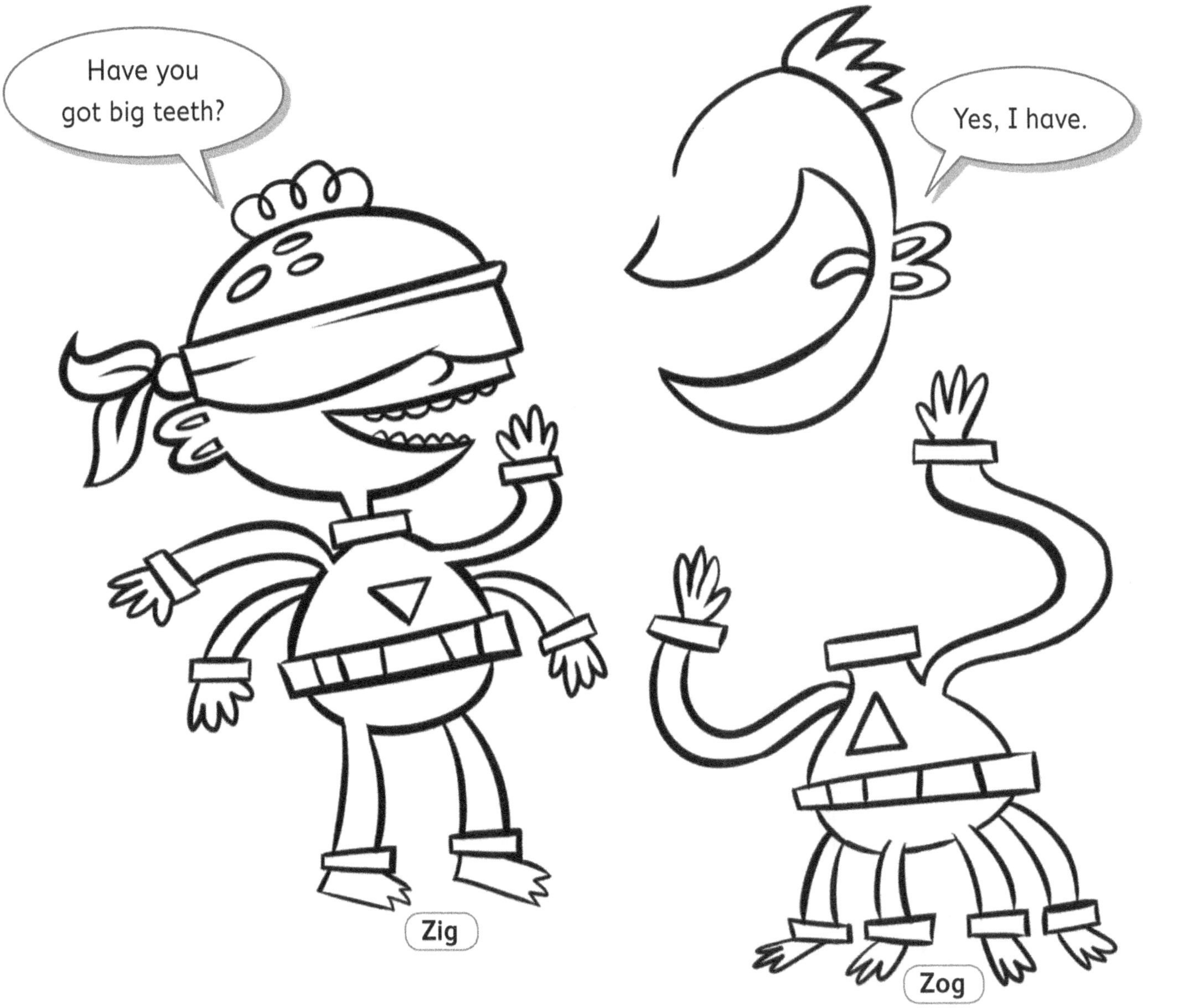

6 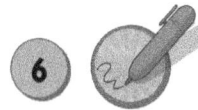 **Write about the aliens.**

Zog has got _four eyes,_ _____.

Zog hasn't got _____.

Zig _____.

_____

7  **Listen, tick (✓) and find the girl.**

① ☐ ✓

Kelly

② ☐ ☐

Laura

③ ☐ ☐

Trudie

8 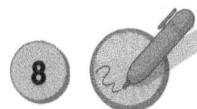 **Now write about the girl. Use the words in the box.**

| black |
| glasses nose |
| She She's |
| teeth |

She's got short ¹____black____ hair.

She's got a small ²_____.

³_____ got big ⁴_____.

⁵_____ hasn't got ⁶_____.

She's ⁷_____!

9 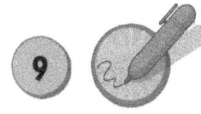 **Rewrite with capital letters and full stops.**

1 he's got short blonde hair

_____

2 he's got big eyes and a small nose

_____

10  **Listen and circle the sound that's different.**

SOUNDS FUN!

1 Sharon   (chair)   sheep   **2** hair   shoe   shape
3 she   ship   they   **4** shell   small   short

11  **Read and number.**

1   He hasn't got a moustache. He's got a hat.

2   She's got long blonde hair and glasses.

3   He's got short black hair.

4   She's got red hair. She hasn't got spots.

12 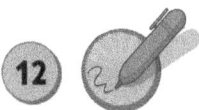   **Number the pictures in order.**

13 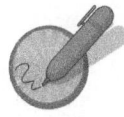 **Complete the diagram. Use the words in the box.**

long tail   big body   big ears   feathers   long legs
long neck   pouch   wings

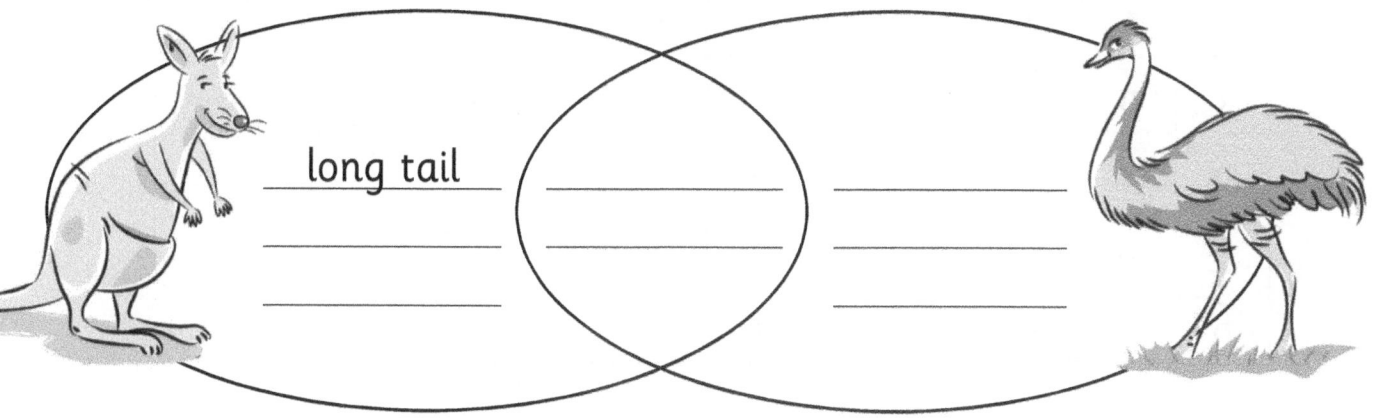

long tail

14  **Read and circle four errors. Then write.**

Kimmy is a koala. She's got (big) eyes and small ears. She hasn't got a pouch. She's got feathers and a tail.

Kimmy

Kimmy's got small eyes, _____.

She hasn't got _____.

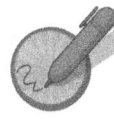 **15** Circle and write the words.

t	e	e	t	h	p	s	b	s
u	m	o	u	s	t	a	e	c
g	l	a	s	s	e	s	a	a
l	n	o	p	e	m	n	r	r
o	s	r	a	c	s	o	d	e
p	o	t	a	p	i	s	o	y
⊂h	a	i	r⊃	h	e	e	e	e
c	a	r	b	n	e	c	k	s
m	o	u	s	t	a	c	h	e

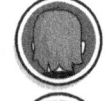 hair _____

 _____

 _____

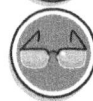 _____

 _____

 _____

 _____

 _____

  **16** Look, find and write the sentences.

1 (beard) (got) (He's) (a)

       He's got a beard.

2 (moustache) (He) (got) (a) (hasn't)

_____

3 (big) (He's) (glasses) (got)

_____

4 (long) (She's) (hair) (got)

_____

5 (got) (hasn't) (glasses) (She)

_____

6 (has) (She) (got) (blonde) (hair)

_____

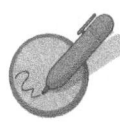 **17** What have you got? Circle.

a beard   long hair

blonde hair   blue eyes

brown eyes   glasses

a moustache   brown hair

short hair   green eyes

a nose   two ears

18 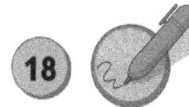 Look and write.

I've got short 🪶 ¹ ___hair___

and brown 👀 ² _____.

I haven't got 👓 ³ _____.

19 Write about yourself. Then tell the class.

I've got _____ hair and _____ eyes.

I haven't got _____.

3 Pets

1 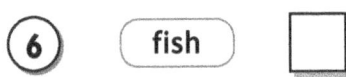 Match.

1 cat [f]
2 frog [ ]
3 dog [ ]
4 snake [ ]
5 parrot [ ]
6 fish [ ]

2 Listen and write.
1:49

We've got a ¹ _____cat_____ and a ² _____. We haven't got a dog.

We've got a ³ _____ , a ⁴ _____ and a ⁵ _____ .

We haven't got a fish.

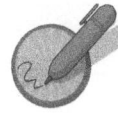

3 **Look and write.**

1 Has it got a big mouth? _____Yes, it has._____

Has it got a tail? _____

What is it? It's a _____.

2 Has it got legs? _____

Has it got two eyes? _____

What is it? It's a _____.

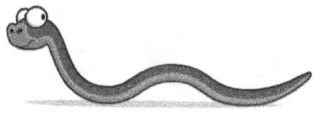

 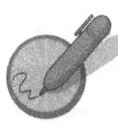

4 **Answer the questions.**

1 Has the cat got wings? _____No, it hasn't._____

2 Has the dog got two eyes? _____

3 Has the parrot got four legs? _____

4 Has the fish got a tail? _____

5 Has the rabbit got ears? _____

6 Has the frog got two legs? _____

5 **Write a description of an animal.**

This is a _____. It's got _____ and

_____ but it hasn't got_____.

6  **Listen and draw.**

① ② ③ ④

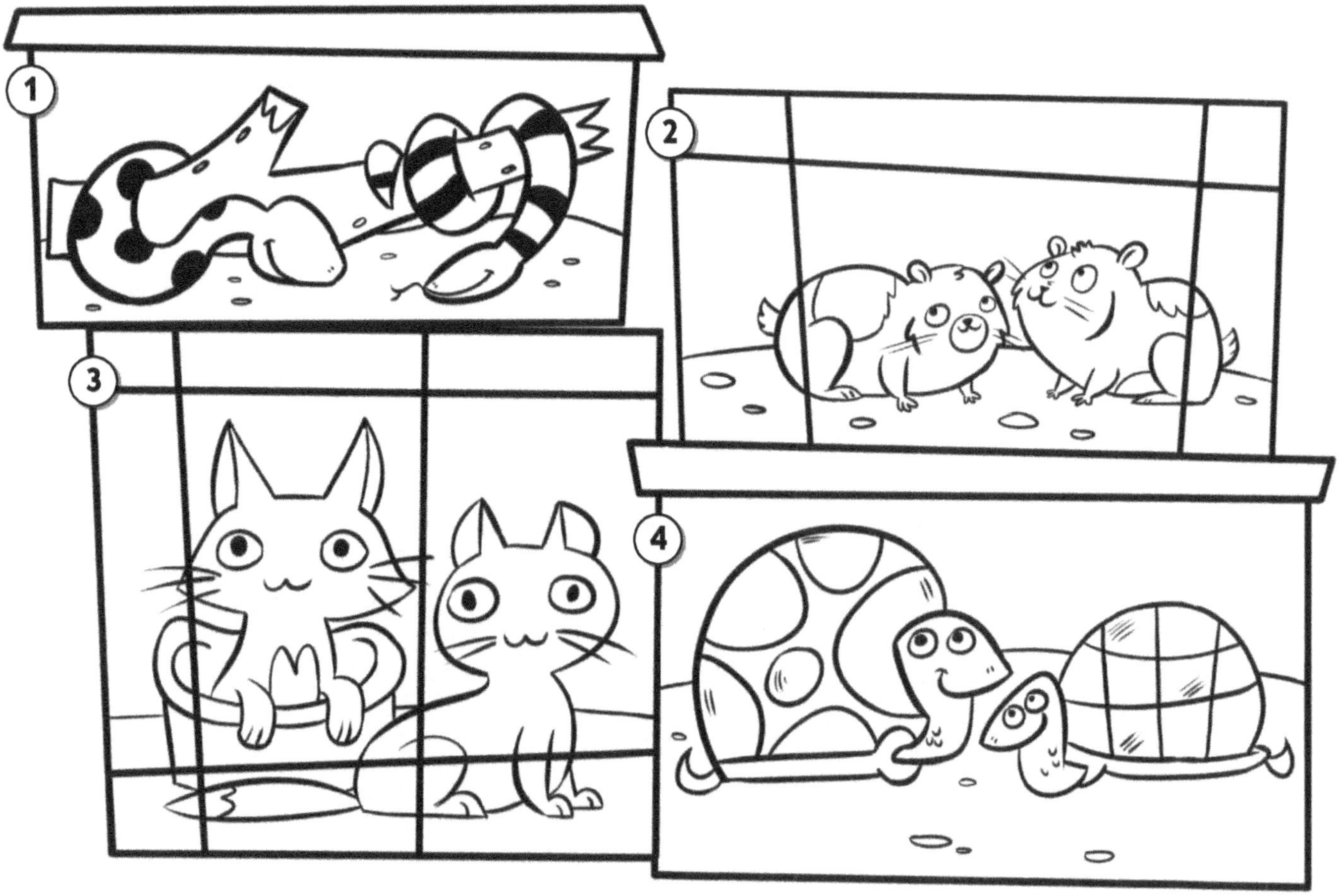

7 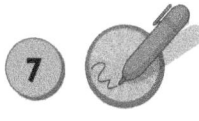 **Answer the questions. What do you think?**
Write *Yes, they have* or *No, they haven't*.

1   Have the cats got pretty noses?   Yes, they have.

2   Have the tortoises got ugly legs?   _____

3   Have the snakes got pretty eyes?   _____

4   Have the tortoises got tails?   _____

5   Have the hamsters got ugly teeth?   _____

6   Have the cats got ugly eyes?   _____

8  **Listen and circle.**

Animal: fish / parrot

Name: Luke / Lily

Home: Australia / South America

Age: 8 years old / 10 years old

Legs: 4 legs / 2 legs

Food: likes apples / likes insects

9 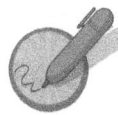 **Read and write. Use the words in the box.**

> apples   eight   legs   Lily   parrot
> pretty   South America   two

Hello, I'm Sophie and I've got a pet. It's a ¹ _____parrot_____ . Its name is
² _____ and it's from ³ _____ . It's ⁴ _____
years old. It hasn't got four ⁵ _____ , it's got ⁶ _____ legs.
It's very ⁷ _____ . It likes ⁸ _____ .

10 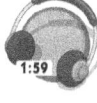 **Listen and write the words in the correct column.**

1	cat	2	snake
3	rat	4	cake
5	lake	6	hat

bat	make
cat	_____
_____	_____
_____	_____

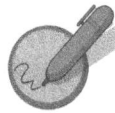 **11** **Look and write *Yes* or *No*.**

Has it got spots? ___Yes___

Has it got a short tail? _____

Has it got sharp teeth? _____

Is it the wabberjock? _____

Is it very big? _____

Has it got long legs? _____

Has it got spots? _____

Is it the wabberjock? _____

Is it small? _____

Has it got spots? _____

Has it got a long tail? _____

Is it the wabberjock? _____

12 **Write about the animals in Activity 11.**

1 This animal has got spots. It's got a long ___tail___ and sharp _____.

2 This animal is very _____. It's got _____ legs and spots.

3 This animal is _____. It's got a _____ tail and spots. It's the wabberjock!

13 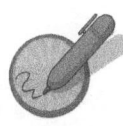 **Number the pictures. Then write.**

SCIENCE

Life cycle of a butterfly

a ☐   b 1   c ☐   d ☐

(butterflies   caterpillars   cocoons   ~~eggs~~)

First, there are small ¹ _____eggs_____ . Next, there ² _____ .

Then ³ _____ . Finally, ⁴ _____ .

14 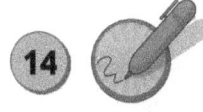 **Look and write. Use the words in the box.**

(big tadpoles   ~~eggs~~   frogs   small tadpoles)

Life cycle of a frog

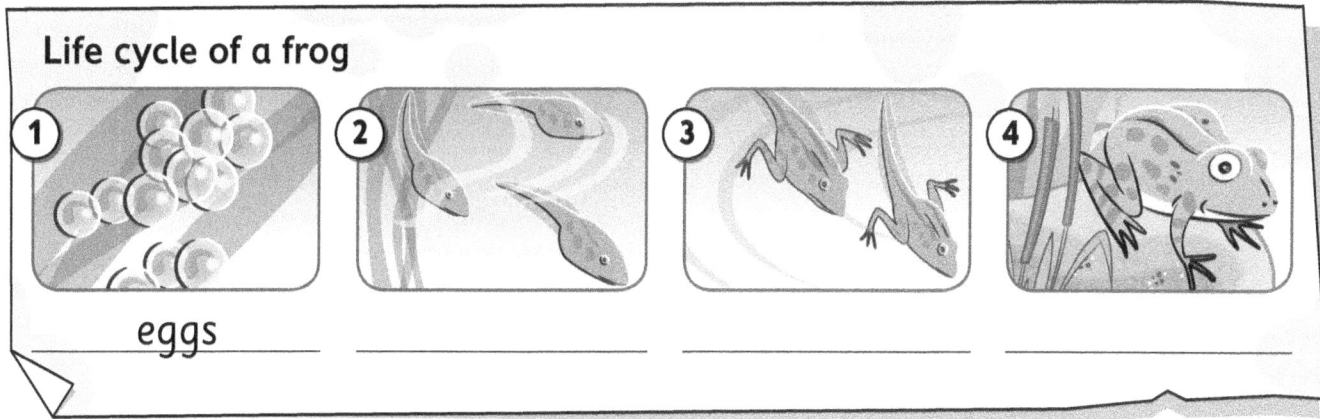

① ② ③ ④

____eggs____   _____   _____   _____

15 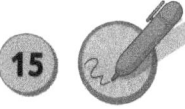 **Answer the questions.**

1   Have butterflies got wings?   _____Yes, they have._____

2   Have frogs got mouths?   _____

3   Have small tadpoles got legs?   _____

4   Have caterpillars got legs?   _____

16  **Look and write.**

cathamstertortoisefrogfishsnakerabbitparrotdog

_____cat_____   _____   _____

_____   _____   _____

_____   _____

17  **Listen and tick (✓).**
1:64

	four legs	short tail	big mouth	big eyes
hamster	✓			
tortoise				
frog				

18  **Write.**

The hamster _has got four legs,_ _____.

The tortoise _____.

The frog _____.

19  Circle the words that describe your favourite pet.

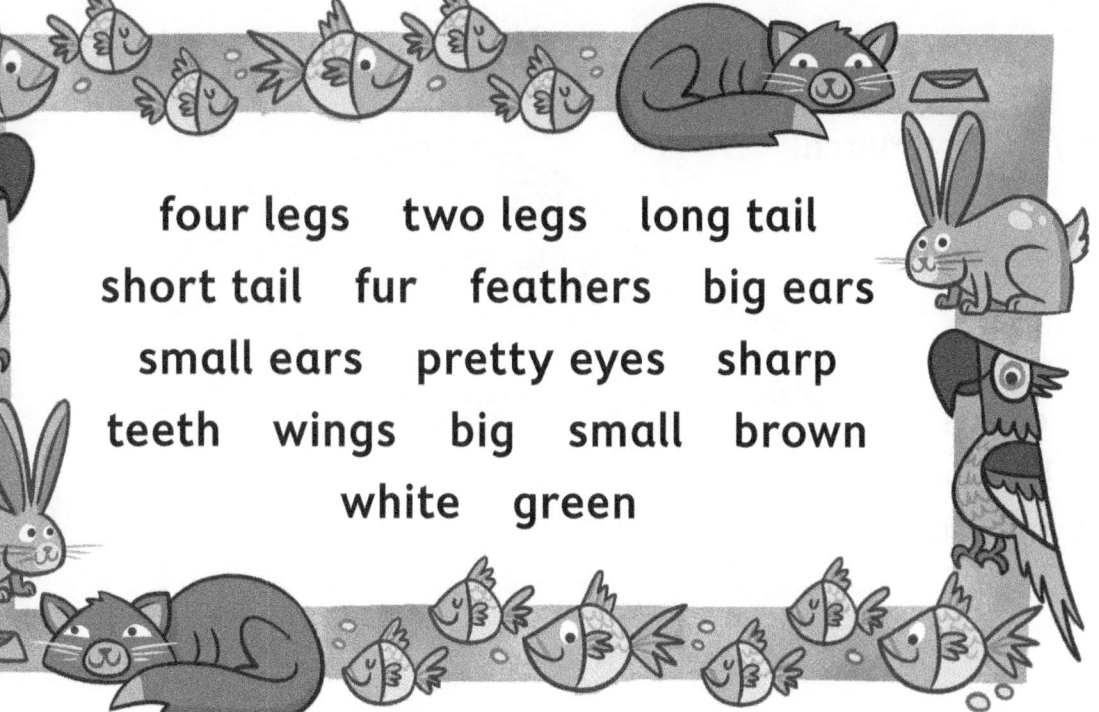

four legs   two legs   long tail
short tail   fur   feathers   big ears
small ears   pretty eyes   sharp
teeth   wings   big   small   brown
white   green

20 Look and write. Use words from activity 19 to complete the sentences.

My favourite pet is a   **1** ___parrot___ . It's red and green.

It's got two   **2** _____ and two   **3** _____.

It hasn't got fur. It's got pretty   **4** _____.

21 Write about your favourite pet. Then tell the class.

My favourite pet is a _____. It's _____.

It's got _____ and _____.

It hasn't got _____.

4 Home

1 Match.

- bathroom
- bed
- bedroom
- cooker
- kitchen
- living room
- shower
- sofa
- TV
- wardrobe

2 Complete the word map.

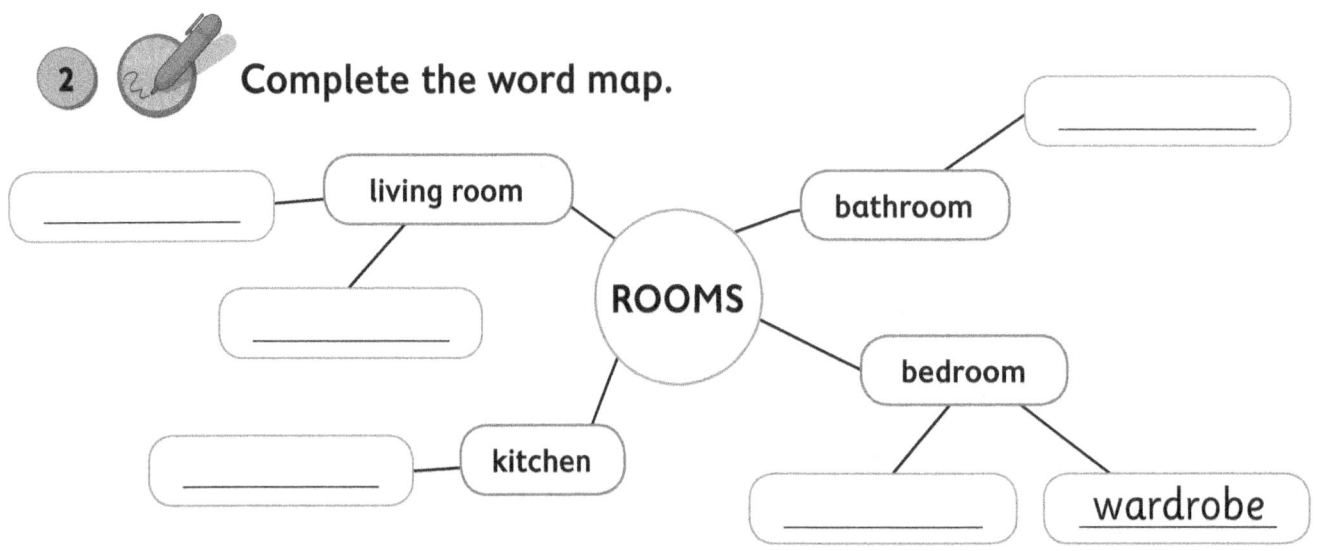

living room

_____

_____

kitchen

ROOMS

bathroom

_____

bedroom

_____   wardrobe

3 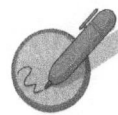 **Look and circle.**

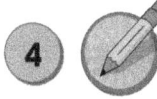

1   Is the cooker in the kitchen?   (Yes, it is. / No, it isn't.)

2   Is the sofa in the bedroom?   (Yes, it is. / No, it isn't.)

3   Is the shower in the bathroom?   (Yes, it is. / No, it isn't.)

4   Is the bed in the living room?   (Yes, it is. / No, it isn't.)

4   **Look at Activity 3 and draw. Then answer.**

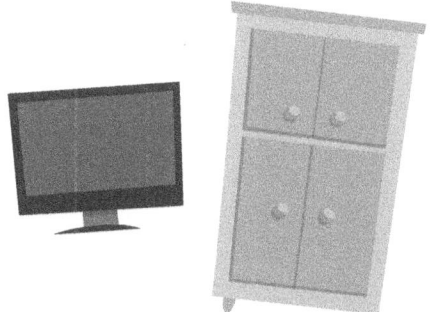

(**Yes, it is.   No, it isn't.**)

1   Is the TV in the living room?

_____

2   Is the wardrobe in the bathroom?

_____

 **5** Where's the frog? Use the words in the box.

 **SONG**

in   on   under

The frog is _____ the bath.

The frog is _____ the lamp.

The frog is _____ the chair.

6 🎧 2:10 **Look and answer. Then listen and check.**

1 Where's the frog? _____ It's on the bed. _____

2 Where's the tortoise? _____

3 Where's the snake? _____

4 Where's the hamster? _____

5 Where's the parrot? _____

6 Where's the rabbit? _____

7  **Listen and write punctuation marks.**

LISTENING

I'm very happy. I've got a great new air chair
It's cool Where's the chair In my bedroom
It's fantastic It's grey and it's got a hamster
on it Where's the hamster It's on the ball
The chair is fun Do you like it

SOUNDS FUN!

8  **Listen and circle the sound that's different.**

1	hot	dog	(school)	**2**	cool	frog	pool
3	frog	cool	dog	**4**	school	pool	hot

9 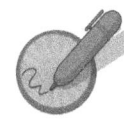 Number the pictures. Then write.
Use the words in the box.

has   got   kitchen   ~~plant~~

a It isn't your plant. It's our ___plant___.

b Oh, no. My _____.

c Have you _____ a tifftiff plant?

d Oh, no! The trickster _____ got the tifftiff plant!

10  Where's the tifftiff plant? Write.

1 It's ___on___ the table.   **2** It's _____ the cooker.

3 It's _____ the wardrobe.   **4** It's _____ the table.

11  **Draw the next four shapes on the frame.
Then colour.**

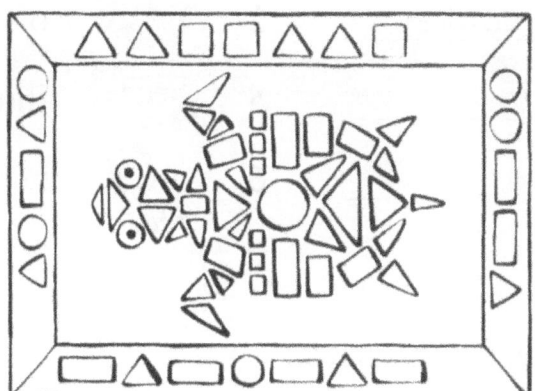

 12  **Write the words. Then draw a mosaic animal.**

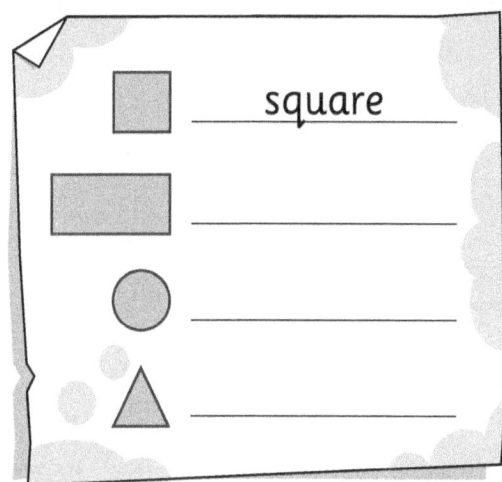

square

_____

_____

_____

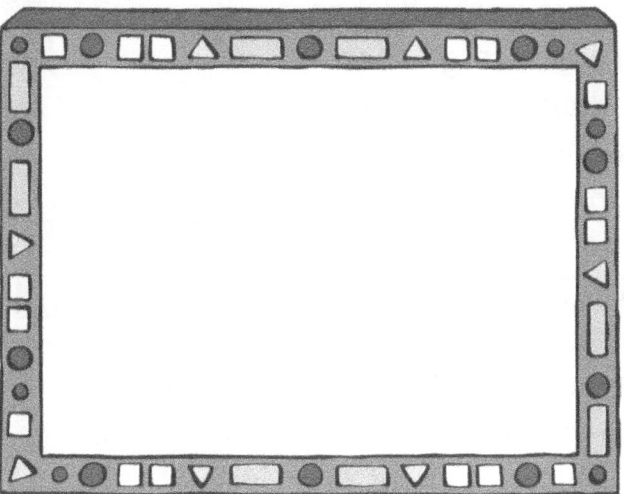

 13  **Count, answer and write.**

1 How many triangles
are there?

2 How many circles
are there?

3 How many squares
are there?

4 How many rectangles
are there?

This is my mosaic animal. It's got _____ squares. It's got _____

_____ .

14 **Find and write the words.**

1  kecoor __cooker__   2  ofsa _____

3  wosher _____   4 thab _____

5 plam _____   6 hcari _____

15 **Read and draw. Then write.**

The cooker and the chair are in the kitchen. There is a frog under the chair. The TV, the sofa and the lamp are in the living room. The lamp is on the table. The bath and the shower are in the bathroom. The bed and the wardrobe are in the bedroom. There are books under the bed.

bedroom

bathroom

kitchen

living room

1 The cooker and the chair are _____in_____ the kitchen.

2 The frog is _____ the chair.

3 The lamp is _____ the table.

4 The bath and shower are _____ the bathroom.

5 The bed is _____ the bedroom.

6 There are books _____ the bed.

16 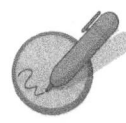 What's in your bedroom? Circle.

my bedroom

bed	books	chair
computer	lamp	shower
sofa	table	TV	wardrobe

17 Look and write.

My favourite room is my bedroom. It's got a  ¹ ___bed___,

a ² _____ and a big ³ _____. There's a

⁴ _____, too. It's on the table.

18 Write about your bedroom. Then tell the class.

My bedroom has got _____ _____.

There's a _____, too. It's _____.

5 Clothes

1 Match.

a trainers
b shirt
c jeans
d cap
e shorts
f tracksuit
g sweatshirt
h jacket
i uniform

2  Listen and tick (✔). Then write.

2:20

a   b   a   b   a   b

✔

1 I'm wearing a ___shirt___, _____ and _____.

2 I'm wearing _____, _____ and a _____.

3 I'm _____ a _____ and a _____.

3  **Listen and draw. Then colour.**

What are you
wearing, Harry?

4 **Now write about Harry.**

Harry's wearing _____ shorts _____, a _____,

_____ and a _____.

5 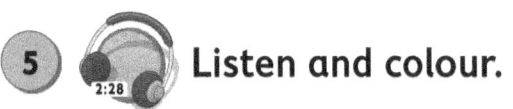 Listen and colour.

6  Read and answer.

> Yes, he/she is.   No, he/she isn't.

1   Is he wearing blue jeans? _____ Yes, he is. _____

2   Is he wearing yellow trainers? _____

3   Is he wearing a blue T-shirt? _____

4   Is she wearing a brown coat? _____

5   Is she wearing a red scarf? _____

6   Is she wearing pink shoes? _____

7   Is she wearing blue socks? _____

7 🎧 2:31 **Listen and tick (✓).**

big shoes	☐
small shoes	☐
big hat	☐
small hat	☐

short skirt	☐
long skirt	☐
big shirt	☐
small shirt	✓

8 ✏️ **What is Hilda wearing? Write.**

Hilda is wearing <u>a small shirt,</u>   .

This is her favourite   .

These are her favourite   .

SOUNDS FUN!

9 🎧 2:32 **Listen and write. Then put the words in the correct column.**

			sh	sk
1	hotsr	<u>short</u>		
2	ysk		**sh**ort	
3	woerhs			
4	pikpers			
5	thirs			
6	rsikt			

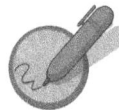 **Look, find and write the sentences.**

's He got tifftiff plant. the
He's got the tifftiff plant.

1

shirt! at Look the red
_____

2

red No, jacket. a it's
_____

3

a dress. wearing is PROD 2
_____

4

 **Look and write.**

1   Is Kim wearing a sweatshirt?   No, he isn't.
                                   _____

2   Is PROD 2 wearing a dress?   _____

3   Is Katy wearing a tracksuit?   _____

4   Is the trickster wearing a cap? _____

12 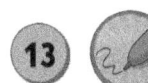 **Match and write.**

1	wash		a	your bedroom		1	wash the dishes
2	make		b	the table		2	
3	tidy		c	the bed		3	
4	lay		d	the dishes		4	

13 **Look at Activity 12 and number.**

a   1

b

c

d   REX

14  **Which chores do you like? Write.**

_____

_____

_____

_____

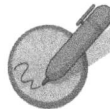 **15** **Circle and write the words.**

What are you wearing?

s	g	z	u	o	s	t	e	k	s
w	c	s	s	c	a	r	f	j	h
e	c	h	l	d	c	a	z	i	o
a	c	i	t	c	l	i	j	i	r
t	f	r	y	o	j	n	e	o	t
s	a	t	h	a	s	e	a	e	s
h	a	t	d	t	o	r	n	e	w
i	f	e	u	z	c	s	s	q	e
r	t	r	a	c	k	s	u	i	t
t	s	h	o	e	s	b	v	q	n

trainers

_____

_____

_____

_____

_____

_____

_____

_____

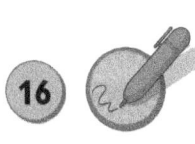 **16** **Correct the sentences.**

1 He is wearing a sweatshirt.

_____He is wearing a T-shirt._____

2 He is wearing trousers.

_____

3 He is wearing shoes.

_____

5

17  **Which clothes have you got? Tick (✓). Then circle your favourite clothes.**

sweatshirt ☐

skirt ☐ dress ☐ jacket ☐

trainers ☐ jeans ☐

scarf ☐ socks ☐ shirt ☐

shoes ☐ hat ☐ T-shirt ☐

trousers ☐ tracksuit ☐

shorts ☐

18  **Look and write.**

My favourite ¹ <u>sweatshirt</u> is red.

My favourite ² _____ are black.

My favourite ³ _____ are blue.

19 **Write about your favourite clothes. Then tell the class.**

My favourite _____ is _____ .

My favourite _____ are _____ .

My favourite _____ .

6 Sports

1 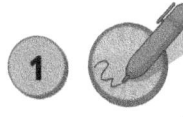 **Match and say.**

a do taekwondo **b** play baseball **c** play basketball
d play football **e** play tennis **f** ride a bike **g** ~~run~~

1 → g

2

3

4

5

6

7

2 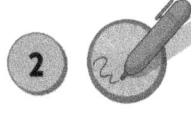 **Look and circle.**

runplaybaseballdotaekwondoplayfootballrideabike

		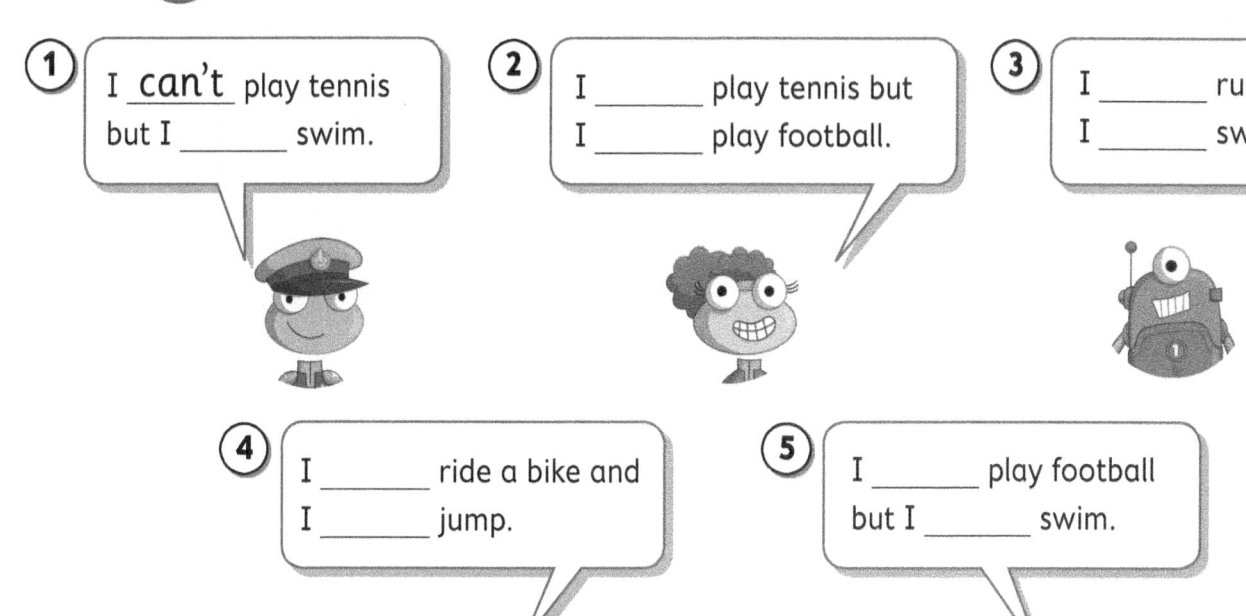					
	Captain Conrad				✓		
	Katy						
	PROD 1						
	PROD 2						
	Kim						

4 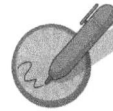 **Write.**

1. I __can't__ play tennis but I _____ swim.

2. I _____ play tennis but I _____ play football.

3. I _____ run but I _____ swim.

4. I _____ ride a bike and I _____ jump.

5. I _____ play football but I _____ swim.

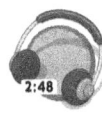 **Listen and tick (✓) or cross (✗).**

6 ✏ **Complete.**

1 Can she _____ play basketball _____? Yes, she can.

2 Can he _____? No, he can't.

3 Can she play tennis? _____

4 Can he jump? _____

7 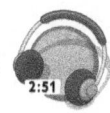 Listen and tick (✓) *can* or cross (✗) *can't*.

 ① ✓

 ②

 ③

 ④

 ⑤

 ⑥

 ⑦

 ⑧

8 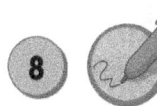 Write *and* or *but*.

Monkeys can run ¹ __and__ jump ² _____ they can't ride a bike. They can swim
³ _____ climb trees ⁴ _____ they can't play tennis. They can catch a ball
⁵ _____ they can't play football.

SOUNDS FUN!

9 Listen and write the words in the correct column.

k	c
mon**k**ey	

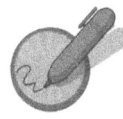 **10** What can PROD 1 and PROD 2 do?
Look and write. Use the words in the box.

> catch   ~~play basketball~~
> play tennis   ride a bike   swim

PROD 1	PROD 2
can play basketball	_____
_____	_____
	_____

 **11** Look and write.

1   PROD 1 _____ can play basketball but he can't run fast _____.

2   PROD 1 _____.

3   PROD 2 _____.

4   PROD 2 _____.

STORY

12  **Listen and number the pictures.**

a [ ]

b [ ]

c [ ]

d [ ]

e [1]

13 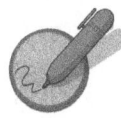 **Make an exercise plan.**
Use the words in the box.

climb trees   ~~dance~~   jump
play basketball
play football   play tennis
ride my bike   run   swim

My exercise plan

Monday	dance
Tuesday	
Wednesday	
Thursday	

Friday	
Saturday	
Sunday	

14  **Write about your exercise plan.**

On Monday, I can dance. On Tuesday, _____

_____

_____

_____ .

15  Match.

> **1** climb trees   **2** jump   **3** play basketball
> **4** play football   **5** play tennis
> **6** ~~ride a bike~~   **7** run   **8** swim

a 6

Ted

b

Sue

c

Lee

d

Liz

16 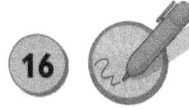 **Look and write.**

1   Ted _____ can swim but he can't ride a bike _____.

2   Sue _____.

3   Lee _____.

4   Liz _____.

17 Tick (✓) the activities you can do. Then circle your favourite sport.

HAVE FUN

run ☐ climb a tree ☐

catch a ball ☐ jump ☐

ride a bike ☐ dance ☐ football ☐

basketball ☐ tennis ☐ baseball ☐

taekwondo ☐ running ☐

swimming ☐ dancing ☐

18 Look and write.

My favourite sport is ¹ _basketball_ .

I can ² _____, ³ _____

and ⁴ _____.

19 Write about your favourite sport. Then tell the class.

My favourite sport is _____. I can _____.

7 Food

1 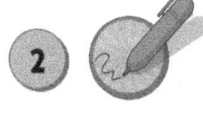 Match.

1. cucumbers
2. strawberries
3. beans
4. peas
5. tomatoes
6. plums
7. potatoes
8. oranges

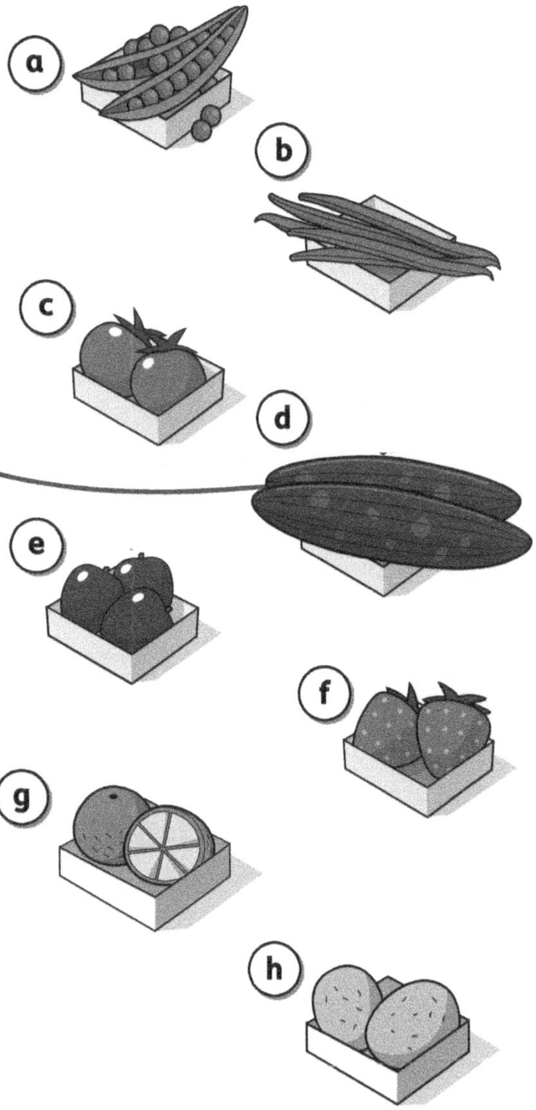

a
b
c
d
e
f
g
h

2 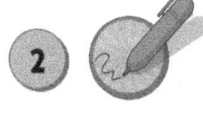 Write about the food you like.

:) I like _____

_____ .

:(I don't like _____

_____ .

 **3** Listen and tick (✓) or cross (✗).

4 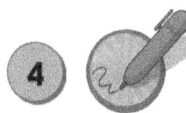 Now write *likes* or *doesn't like*.

1 She _____likes_____ strawberries.   **2** She _____ plums.

3 She _____ peas.   **4** He _____ cucumbers.

5 He _____ beans.   **6** He _____ tomatoes.

 **5** **Look and answer.**

Does he/she like...	Tim	Liz
peaches?	✓	✓
potatoes?	✓	✗
cucumbers?	✗	✓
carrots?	✗	✗
beans?	✗	✗
plums?	✓	✓
strawberries?	✓	✗
peas?	✗	✓

1 Does Tim like beans? _____ No, he doesn't. _____

2 Does he like potatoes? _____

3 Does he like cucumbers? _____

4 Does Liz like peaches? _____

5 Does she like carrots? _____

6 Does she like strawberries? _____

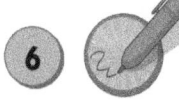 **6** **Write about Tim and Liz.**

Tim likes _peaches, _____.

He doesn't like _____.

Liz likes _____.

She doesn't like _____.

7  Listen and draw a happy or sad face.

8 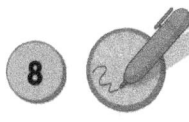 **Look and write.**

1 Does he like cereal? <u>Yes, he does.</u>

2 Does he like strawberries? _____

3 Does he like eggs and toast? _____

4 Does he like peaches? _____

5 _____ bananas? Yes, he does.

6 _____ plums? No, he doesn't.

9  **Listen and write *p* or *b*.**

 b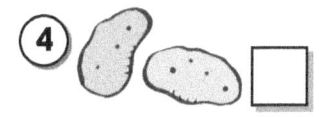

  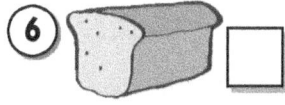   

10 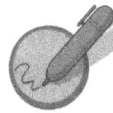 **Look at the story again. Write.**

1. Kim, do you like __strawberries__ ?

2. No, I _____ like eggs!

3. I _____ tifftiff plants!

4. He _____ like tifftiff plants!

11 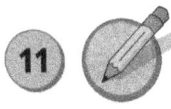 **Draw food you like below YUM and food you don't like below YUCK. Then write.**

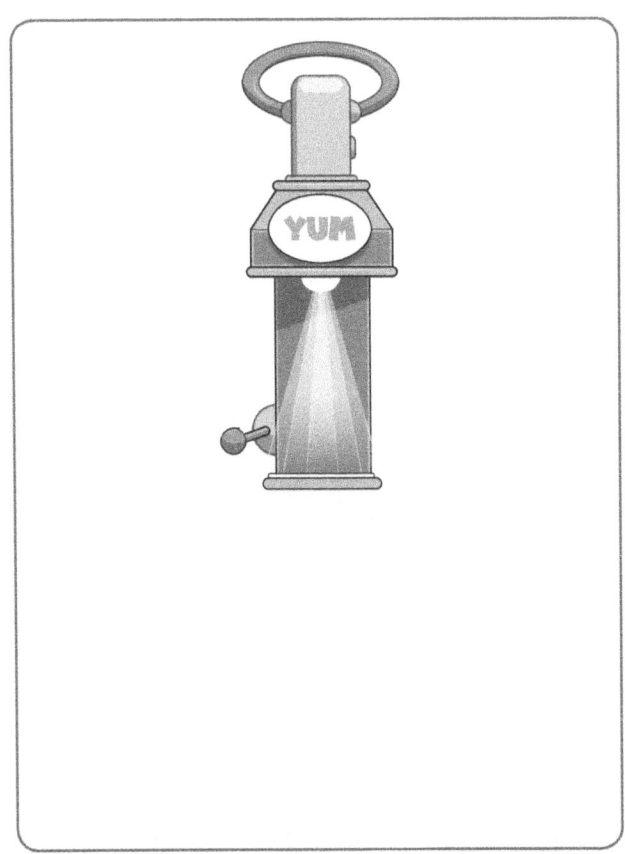

I like _____.

I don't like _____.

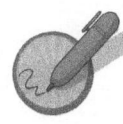 **12** Choose and write five healthy snacks.

13 Draw three healthy meals. Use food from the healthy food plate.

breakfast   lunch   dinner

14 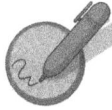 Now write about your three healthy meals.

For breakfast, I like _____.

For lunch, I like _____.

For dinner, I like _____.

15 Complete the crossword.

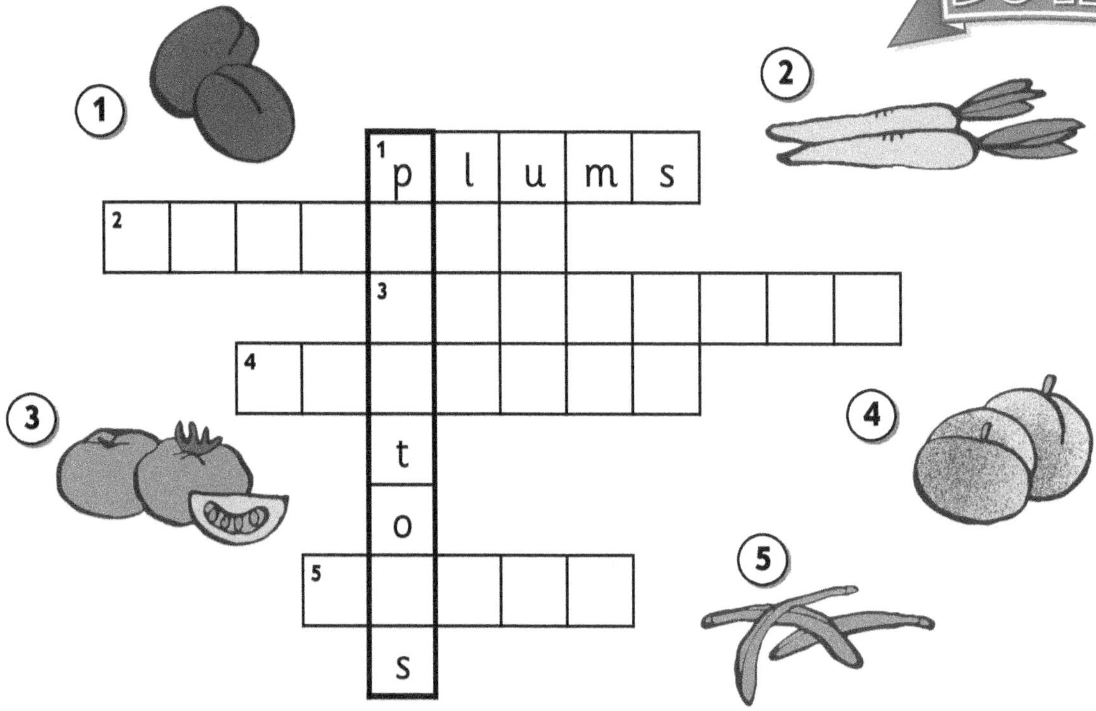

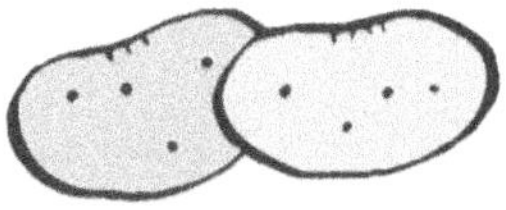

①

②

③

④

⑤

```
  1 p  l  u  m  s
2 [  ][  ][  ][  ]
  3 [  ][  ][  ][  ][  ][  ][  ]
  4 [  ][  ][  ]
      t
      o
5 [  ][  ][  ][  ]
      s
```

What word can you find? p _ _ _ _ _ _ _ _

16 Look and answer.

1 Does he like beans?   Yes, he does.

2 Does he like carrots?   _____

3 Does he like potatoes?   _____

4 Does he like peas?   _____

17 Write.

He likes carrots _____.

He doesn't like _____.

58 Lesson 7

18  **What do you like? Tick (✓) and cross (✗). Then circle your favourite food.**

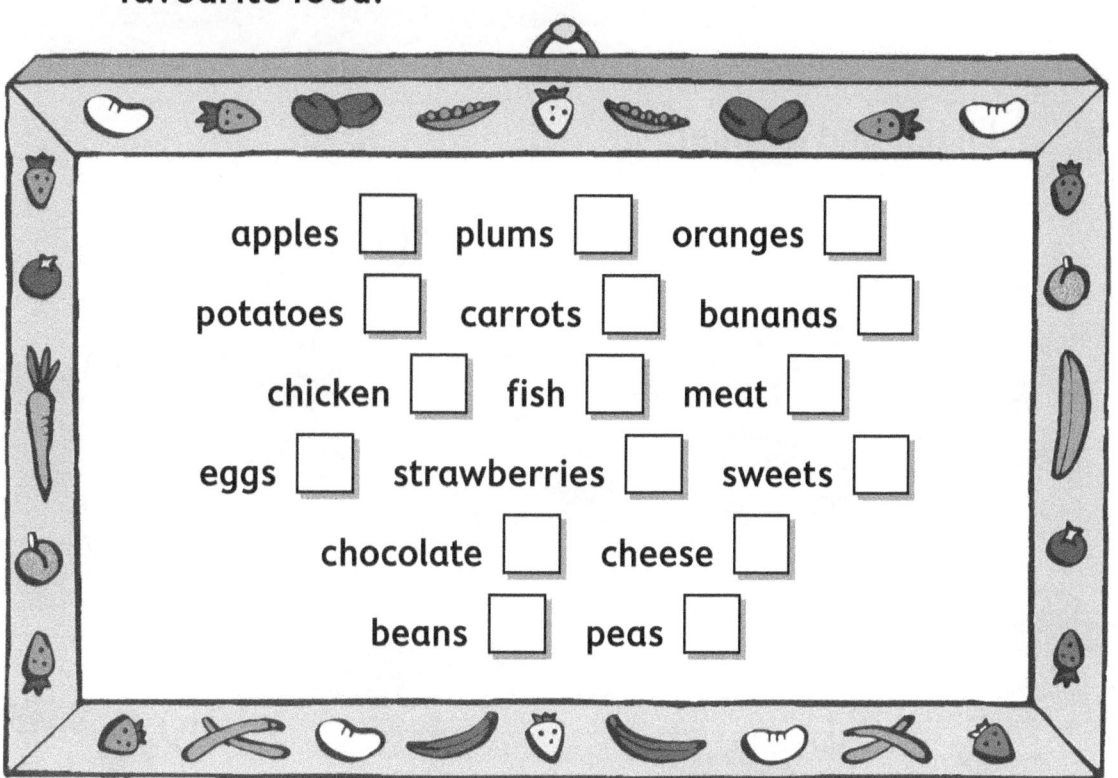

apples ☐   plums ☐   oranges ☐

potatoes ☐   carrots ☐   bananas ☐

chicken ☐   fish ☐   meat ☐

eggs ☐   strawberries ☐   sweets ☐

chocolate ☐   cheese ☐

beans ☐   peas ☐

19 **Look and write.**

I like ¹ __strawberries__ , ² _____

and ³ _____ .

I love ⁴ _____ . They're good for me. Yum!

20 **Write about your favourite food. Is it healthy? Then tell the class.**

I like _____ , _____ and _____ .

I love _____ . _____ . Yum!

1 🎧 **3:22** **Listen and number.**

a

b

c

d

e 1

f

g

h

2 ✏️ **Now look and write. Use the words in the box.**

cleaning   dancing   doing homework   drinking   eating
listening to music   reading   sleeping

Picture a _____cleaning_____   Picture b _____

Picture c _____   Picture d _____

Picture e _____   Picture f _____

Picture g _____   Picture h _____

3 🎧 **3:26** **Listen, read and match.**

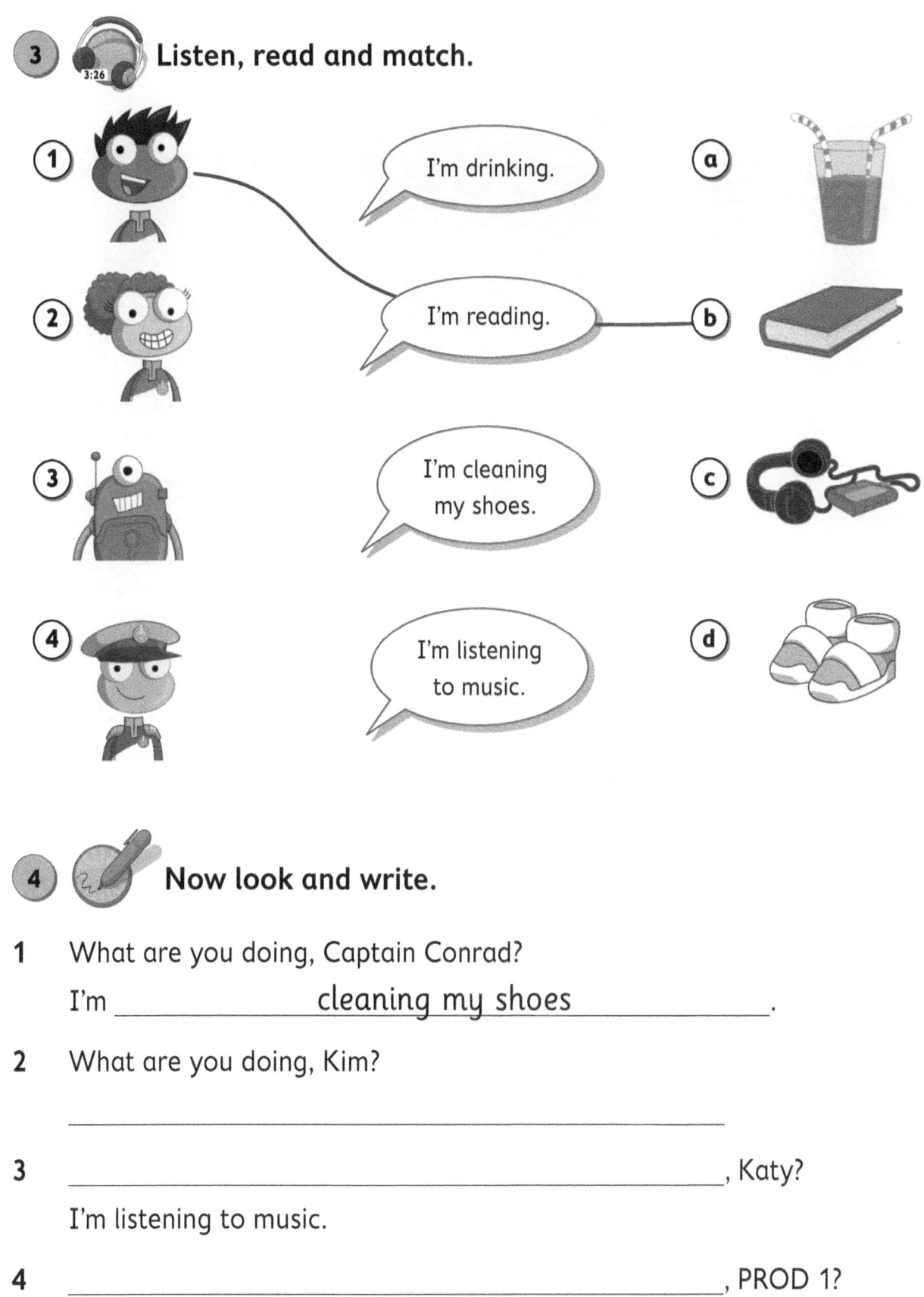

1 I'm drinking. **a**

2 I'm reading. **b**

3 I'm cleaning my shoes. **c**

4 I'm listening to music. **d**

4 ✏️ **Now look and write.**

1 What are you doing, Captain Conrad?
I'm _____ cleaning my shoes _____.

2 What are you doing, Kim?
_____

3 _____, Katy?
I'm listening to music.

4 _____, PROD 1?
_____

5  Listen and tick (✓) or cross (✗).

 ✓

6 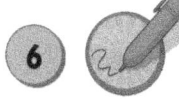 Write the questions. Then answer.

Yes, I am.   No, I'm not.

1   (you) (Are) (jumping)   <u>Are you jumping?</u>   <u>Yes, I am.</u>

2   (running) (Are) (you)   _____   _____

3   (you) (walking) (Are)   _____   _____

4   (swimming) (you) (Are)   _____   _____

5   (Are) (sleeping) (you)   _____   _____

6   (you) (drinking) (Are)   _____   _____

7  **Listen and complete the postcard.**  LISTENING

Hi...

I'm in Spain, at the beach. It's great and it's hot! I'm ¹___eating___ a ² _____ by the pool.

My sister is ³ _____ and Mum ⁴ _____ ⁵ _____.

See you soon!

Bye,

Adam

To: _____

_____

_____

_____

_____

 **Now listen and write the address.**

10 Hill Street
W1G 9DQ
Mr and Mrs Smith
England
London

8  **Listen and match.** SOUNDS FUN!

1
3
5

a (reading)

b (walking)

c (sleeping)

d (eating)

e (drinking)

f (swimming)

2

4

6

9 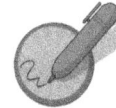 **Look and match.**

a I'm flying home.

b I'm gardening.

c I'm running.

10  **Look and write. Use the words in the box.**

flying   listening   reading   sleeping

Captain Conrad's ¹ _____ flying _____ the spaceship. Katy's

² _____ a book about plants. Kim is ³ _____

to music. PROD 1 is ⁴ _____ . PROD 2 is sleeping, too.

11  **Listen, draw and colour.**

12  **Look and write. Use the words in the box.**

cap   fast   ~~flying~~   pilot   wings

This is a plane. It's ¹_____flying_____ in
the sky. It can fly very ²_____.
It's white and grey. It's got two big
³_____ and two small wings.
A ⁴_____ is flying the plane.
He's wearing a ⁵_____.

13  **Complete the crossword.**

1. ¹s w i m m i n g
   l
2.
3.
   p
4.
5.
   g

What word can you find?   s _ _ _ _ _ _ _

14 **Write. Use the words in the box.**

~~running~~   jumping   swimming   walking

What are you doing?

1 I'm running.

2 _____

3 _____

4 _____

I CAN DO IT!

66   Lesson 7

15  What do you like? Circle. Draw your favourite activity.

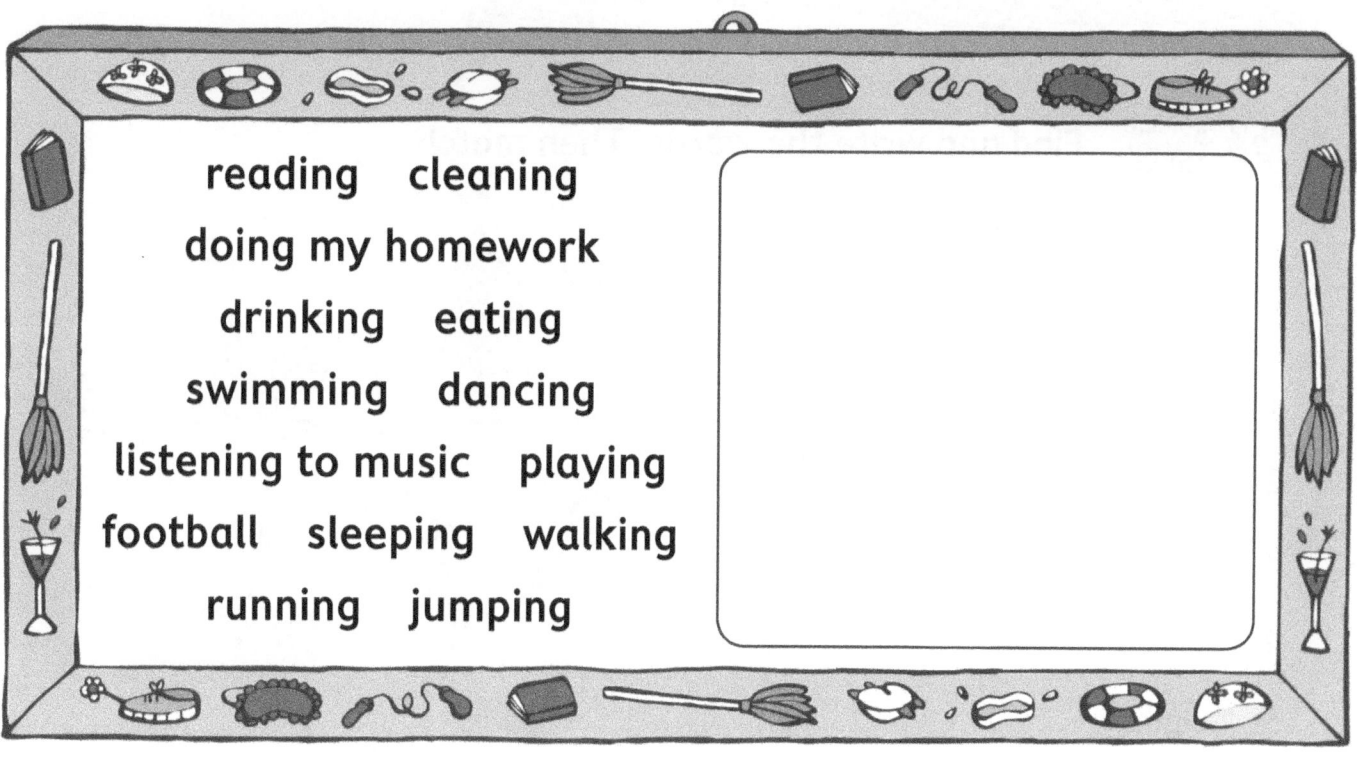

reading   cleaning

doing my homework

drinking   eating

swimming   dancing

listening to music   playing

football   sleeping   walking

running   jumping

16  Look and write.

Look at my picture. I'm 🏃⚽ ¹ <u>playing football</u>.

I'm wearing my 👟 ² _____.

I'm in the 🏞 ³ _____.

17  Write about your picture. Answer the questions. Then tell the class.

1   What are you doing?   _____

2   What are you wearing?   _____

3   Where are you?   _____

Christmas

1 Find and write the words. Then match.

1 gctoiskns   stockings

2 srmtshCia erte _____

3 sarcd   _____

4 antSa   _____

5 siglht   _____

6 nepstres   _____

2  Listen, draw and colour. Then write.

I've got a lot of Christmas presents. I've got a big red bike, _____

_____ .

1  **Look and write.**

①  ②  ③  ④

Easter basket _____ _____ _____

2 🎧 **3:51** **Find the Easter eggs. Listen, draw and colour.**

3 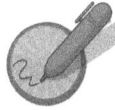 **Look at Activity 2. Write and match.**

blue green pink purple red

1   The blue egg is _____ on the
2   _____ under the
3   _____ in the
4   _____ on the
5   _____ under the

Picture dictionary

Nature

flowers

rock

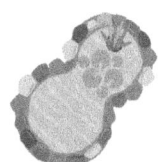
pond

birds

animal

insects

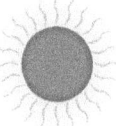
sun

mushrooms

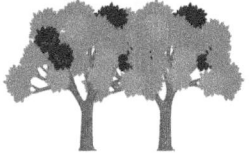
trees

clouds

Me

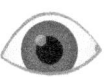

eyes

blonde hair

glasses

short hair

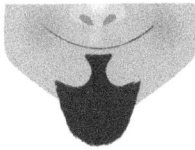
beard

moustache

nose

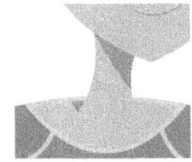
neck

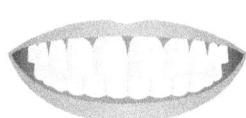
teeth

Animals

cat

frog

fish

rabbit

parrot

snake

dog

tortoise

hamster

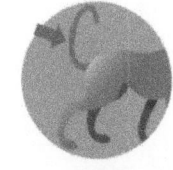
tail

Home

 bed

 cooker

 wardrobe

 TV

 shower

 sofa

 bath

 chair

 lamp

Clothes

 trainers

 uniform

 shirt

 jeans

 jacket

 cap

 tracksuit

 shorts

 sweatshirt

 scarf

 socks

 coat

Sports

 run

 ride a bike

 play tennis

 jump

 do taekwondo

 swim

 play football

 play basketball

 play baseball

 catch a ball

 climb a tree

Food

 peas

 beans

 oranges

 tomatoes

 cucumbers

plums

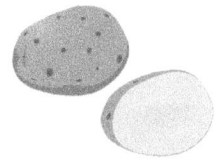 strawberries

 potatoes

carrots

 peaches

Things we do

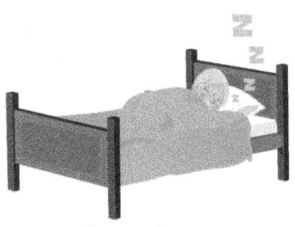
sleeping

reading

eating

drinking

cleaning

doing homework

dancing

listening to music

jumping

swimming

walking

running

Christmas

Santa

Christmas tree

cards

lights

stockings

presents

Easter

Easter bunny

Easter basket

ribbon

Easter egg